Thunder Lizards
Coloring Book
Volume 1

by

Brynda Dunbar

Title: Thunder Lizards Coloring Book Volume 1

ISBN 9798323180332

Copyright 2024 Brynda Dunbar

Thank You

I am Brynda Dunbar and I am a Coloring Book Artist and Creator. I create Coloring Books for all ages. My works have been used for Preschool children, Adults and even an people with dementia. Coloring has been known to induce Stress Relief and Relaxation.

Scan the QR Code below and it will take you to my Amazon Author Page where you can view all the current books that are available. I frequently add new content.

If you like what you see, please follow me, this will let you know when something new is added.

Thank you for taking the time to explore the wonderful world of coloring.

Brynda Dunbar

This book belongs to:

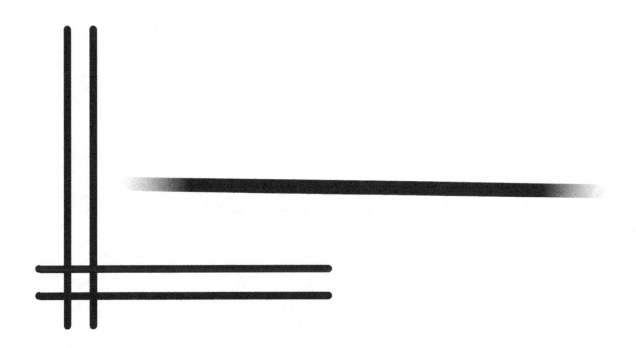

This page is for testing out media that you will be using in this book. I am placing a dark blank page after each design to assist with bleeding. If you want to make sure that there is no bleed thru, I would suggest that you place a piece of paper or cardstock behind the page to help prevent bleed thru.

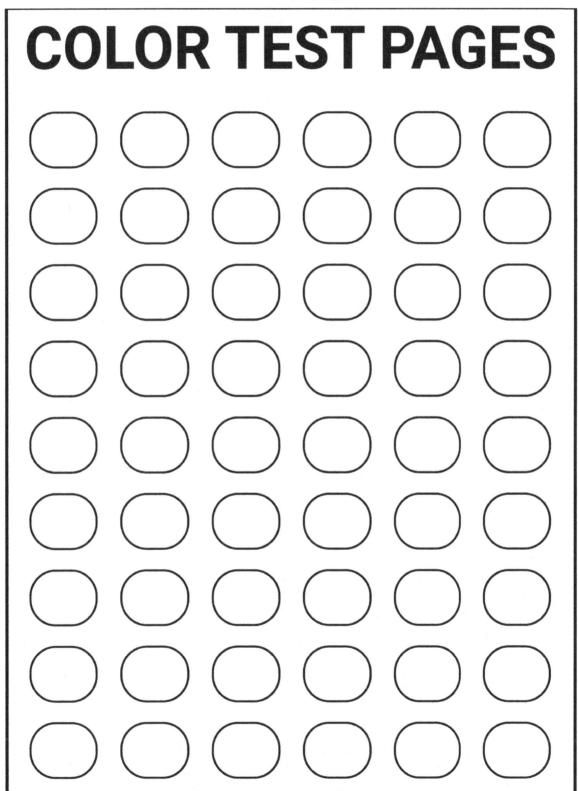

COLOR TEST PAGES

Congratulations
Good job

NAME:

**You have completed
this book with
new skills!!!!!!**

KEEP UP
THE GOOD
WORK

Thank You

Thank you for your purchase! If you have enjoyed this book, please consider dropping us a review. It takes 5 seconds and helps small businesses like ours.

The QR Code below will take you to your purchase page.

Brynda Dunbar

Made in the USA
Las Vegas, NV
02 December 2024

13170983R00063